INSIDE MLS

MINNESOTA UNITED FC

BY CHRÖS MCDOUGALL

SportsZone
An Imprint of Abdo Publishing
abdobooks.com

abdobooks.com

Published by Abdo Publishing, a division of ABDO, PO Box 398166, Minneapolis, Minnesota 55439. Copyright © 2022 by Abdo Consulting Group, Inc. International copyrights reserved in all countries. No part of this book may be reproduced in any form without written permission from the publisher. SportsZone™ is a trademark and logo of Abdo Publishing.

Printed in the United States of America, North Mankato, Minnesota
052021
092021

THIS BOOK CONTAINS RECYCLED MATERIALS

Cover Photo: Joe Petro/Icon Sportswire
Interior Photos: Orlin Wagner/AP Images, 4–5; Andy Witchger/Used under CC 2.0/Edited from original, 6–7; Carlos Gonzalez/Star Tribune/AP Images, 9, 11, 12; Jim Mone/AP Images, 15; David Brewster/Star Tribune/Getty Images, 17; Martin Levison/Star Tribune/Getty Images, 18; Bruce Bisping/Star Tribune/AP Images, 21; Leila Navidi/Star Tribune/AP Images, 22, 32; William Purnell/Icon Sportswire/AP Images, 25; Aaron Lavinsky/Star Tribune/AP Images, 27; Jeff Wheeler/Star Tribune/AP Images, 28, 31; Elizabeth Flores/Star Tribune/AP Images, 35; Alex Kormann/Star Tribune/AP Images, 36; Rich Graessle/Icon Sportswire/AP Images, 38; Andy Clayton-King/AP Images, 41, 42

Editor: Patrick Donnelly
Series Designer: Dan Peluso

Library of Congress Control Number: 2020948263

Publisher's Cataloging-in-Publication Data

Names: McDougall, Chrös, author.
Title: Minnesota United FC / by Chrös McDougall
Description: Minneapolis, Minnesota : Abdo Publishing, 2022 | Series: Inside MLS | Includes online resources and index.
Identifiers: ISBN 9781532194757 (lib. bdg.) | ISBN 9781098214418 (ebook)
Subjects: LCSH: Minnesota United FC (Soccer team)--Juvenile literature. | Soccer teams--Juvenile literature. | Professional sports franchises--Juvenile literature. | Sports Teams--Juvenile literature.
Classification: DDC 796.334--dc23

TABLE OF CONTENTS

CHAPTER 1
TAKING FLIGHT 4

CHAPTER 2
COME TOGETHER 14

CHAPTER 3
LOON CALL 24

CHAPTER 4
LEARNING TO SOAR 34

TIMELINE	44
TEAM FACTS	45
GLOSSARY	46
MORE INFORMATION	47
ONLINE RESOURCES	47
INDEX	48
ABOUT THE AUTHOR	48

CHAPTER 1

TAKING FLIGHT

Ozzie Alonso was heated. The Minnesota United FC captain charged into the locker room, grabbed a plastic bottle, and threw it. The September 25, 2019, game against Sporting Kansas City was not going as planned.

The Loons, as Minnesota United is called, had come out flat. Early in the first half, Kansas City's Botond Barath put his team up 1–0. Even worse, the ball appeared to bounce off Barath's arm, but the referee missed it. Now the Loons were trailing at halftime of a game they needed to win. A victory, after all, would secure the team's first Major League Soccer (MLS) playoff berth.

Minnesota United defender Ike Opara, left, battles Sporting Kansas City's Erik Hurtado for a header.

HOME AT LAST

Men's pro soccer is hardly new in Minnesota. The Twin Cities had a popular first-division team in the 1970s. One team or another has represented the area continuously since 1990. Those teams had mostly played in minor leagues, though. What was new was MLS.

Minnesota United had moved up to the country's top league in 2017. But the first two years were often a struggle. Playing home games at an oversized college football stadium, the Loons gave up a league-record 70 goals that first season. Then they gave up 71 in 2018.

Minnesota United fans were excited to follow the club to their gleaming new stadium in St. Paul.

Still, the 2019 season brought reason for hope. Several talented players, including Alonso, had joined the team that offseason. The team was opening a brand new soccer-specific stadium called Allianz Field in St. Paul. And on April 13, 2019, Loons fans got their first in-person look at the team and stadium when New York City Football Club (FC) came to town for the home opener. In the match's 13th minute, the ball came Alonso's way. With a hard-hit volley, he sent the ball crashing into the net for the first goal in Allianz Field. Although the Loons ended up tying the game 3–3, their future had never looked brighter.

A PROVEN LEADER

As a young player, Osvaldo "Ozzie" Alonso wanted to leave his native Cuba. The government wouldn't let him, however, so he defected to the United States. In 2008 Alonso was playing for a minor league team when the Seattle Sounders discovered him. Over 10 seasons there, the defensive midfielder proved to be one of MLS' toughest—and most respected—players. Minnesota, seeking a strong leader, signed him in 2019.

Allianz Field was instantly one of the league's iconic stadiums. A curved outer skin made it look like a giant spaceship from the outside. At night these walls could be lit up to glow in different colors. Inside, Allianz Field had seating for 19,400. However, the most passionate fans who watch from the steep supporters' section on the south end don't do much sitting during the games. Fans were also proud that the team didn't ask the local community to help pay for the stadium, as many pro sports teams do. Instead, the team owners covered the cost of the $250 million soccer-specific stadium themselves. And located halfway between downtown Minneapolis and downtown St. Paul, it was a perfect home for a team called United.

Minnesota recorded its first win at the new stadium on April 28, defeating DC United 1–0. And the Loons continued to rack up wins after that. Before long, they were in position to lock up a playoff berth. However, in the first opportunity

Ozzie Alonso brought toughness and leadership to the Loons.

to do so, United tied 0–0 on the road at Portland. Now, three days later, the Loons trailed a struggling Kansas City team at the half. Alonso, who had never missed the playoffs in 10 MLS seasons, wasn't about to let that streak end.

THE COMEBACK

The Loons were in need of a spark. Coach Adrian Heath provided one, subbing in speedy forward Abu Danladi and rookie midfielder Hassani Dotson. Soon Minnesota began to take control of the game. Then, in the 70th minute, Alonso struck. When the ball deflected his way on a corner kick, the 33-year-old defensive midfielder smashed a volley into the back of the net. It was only his second goal of the season, and like the first one, it couldn't have come at a better time.

Neither team was going to be satisfied with a draw, though. Each took turns attacking the other end. Vito Mannone made sure Kansas City stopped there. The Minnesota goalkeeper was on fire after giving up Sporting's early score. He smothered, batted away, or cleared any ball that came near him.

United wasn't having much luck either, however. With time running out, the teams remained deadlocked. A draw would mean the playoff berth would have to wait. The sellout crowd at Allianz Field weren't interested in waiting. Neither were the Loons.

As the clock ticked toward the 90th minute, Alonso sent a long pass to Dotson at the top right corner of the penalty area. Dotson turned toward the center of the field. Three KC

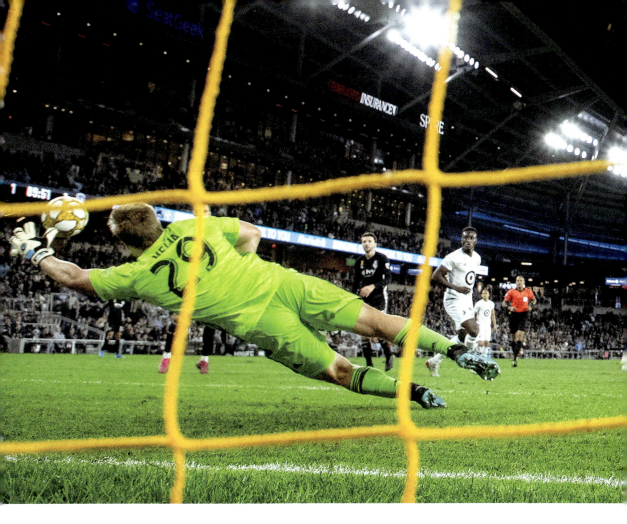

Hassani Dotson's shot slips past the Kansas City goalkeeper and into the net.

defenders had a chance to stop him. Dotson dribbled around each of them. Just beyond the penalty spot, he unleashed a left-footed shot. The ball bounced off a defender's back and flew safely into the net. The packed supporters' section behind the goal roared in approval. And after five more minutes of stoppage time, the whistle blew. Minnesota United had a 2–1 victory, and the Loons were headed to the playoffs.

Dotson celebrates his huge goal that gave the Loons their first playoff berth.

Before the Minnesota faithful could go home, however, there was one more tradition to partake in. Fans stood at their seats. Many raised their scarves. Then, together with the players on the field, they belted out their victory song, "Wonderwall." The moment was as much a celebration for the fans as for the players. After a long history in the minor leagues, and then two challenging seasons at the top level, Minnesota's soccer team was headed to the MLS playoffs.

"We've come a long way," central defender Michael Boxall said, "and they've been there for us the whole time, through thick and thin."

WONDERWALL

Throughout the 2011 season, Minnesota Stars assistant coach Carl Craig could often be found singing the song "Wonderwall" by Oasis. When the team clinched the league's final playoff berth, everyone belted out the anthem together. A videographer happened to capture the moment. As the minor league team ended up making a magical run to the league championship that season, the fans joined in on the postgame tradition. The Stars later became Minnesota United. And now the fans stand and sing "Wonderwall" together after each Loons win.

CHAPTER 2

COME TOGETHER

So many people showed up to Metropolitan Stadium on August 25, 1976, that they ran out of seats to sit in. The Twins baseball team didn't have a home game that night, though. And the Vikings football season hadn't yet started. Instead, the league-record crowd of 49,572 was there to see the Minnesota Kicks soccer team. And after the Kicks defeated the San Jose Earthquakes 3–1, many of those fans ran onto the field to celebrate. In the first year of major pro soccer in Minnesota, the Kicks were headed to the North American Soccer League (NASL) championship game.

While soccer grew around the world in the 20th century, other sports proved to be more popular in the United States. That began to change, albeit briefly, during the NASL years.

Minnesota Kicks goalkeeper Geoff Barnett, bottom, dives to smother a ball as Los Angeles forward Steve David avoids making contact in a 1977 NASL game.

The league was founded in 1968. New teams were added over the next several years. The league also attracted some of the world's most famous players. And prior to that 1976 season, the Denver Dynamos moved to Minnesota and became the Kicks.

Long before the site became the Mall of America, Met Stadium in Bloomington was home to the Twins, Vikings, and Kicks. The Kicks crowds, mostly young people, were taken by the sport. Cheap tickets, pregame tailgating, and a carnival atmosphere helped. The Kicks also proved to be pretty good. As a result, Minnesota had one of the league's most popular teams. Only two NASL teams ever averaged at least 30,000 fans across a season. The Kicks did so twice.

However, poor management doomed the Kicks. After the 1981 season, the struggling team folded. Three years later, the league itself went under. It proved to be the end of an era, though the foundation had been set for soccer to grow in the Twin Cities.

BUZZ AND THE THUNDER

Buzz Lagos came up with an idea. The boys' soccer coach at St. Paul Academy, an elite private high school in the state's capital city, knew the Twin Cities area had many talented players. So in 1990, he helped put together an amateur team

Buzz Lagos was a key figure in bringing pro soccer back to Minnesota.

called the Thunder. It wasn't the first local team since the Kicks folded. A team called the Strikers had played the NASL's final season in 1984, then continued on four more years as an indoor team. However, the Thunder's founding marked an important

Dustin Branan of the Thunder fires a shot on goal against Edmonton in a 2004 match.

milestone. Although the leagues and team names changed over the years, the Twin Cities have been home to a men's soccer team ever since.

The Thunder became a pro team in 1995, joining the A-League. Over the years they played mostly at the National Sports Center in Blaine, a suburb just north of Minneapolis. The team had some success. In 1999 the Thunder won the league championship. Local players went on to bigger things, too.

Tony Sanneh later starred for the United States at the 2002 World Cup. Manny Lagos—Buzz's son—played in the 1992 Olympics and later in MLS. He has held various roles with the Thunder and United since then.

In 2009, however, the sport's future in Minnesota was in doubt. The Thunder was losing money. Then its owner left without paying the team's bills. That ended the rich history of the Thunder. But a new era was beginning.

TAKING THE NEXT STEP

Somebody needed to step up if Minnesota was to have a pro men's soccer team in 2010. The National Sports Center did just that. It created a new team called the Stars. They picked up where the Thunder left off, just with a new name and uniform. However, after one season, the league took ownership of the team. It hoped to quickly find a new owner who was wealthy enough to support the team. But no one immediately stepped up.

Nicknamed by fans as "The Team That Nobody Wanted," the Stars put together a memorable run. They won the league championship in 2011, then reached the championship again the next year. But time was running out to find a new owner.

Earlier that summer, however, a local businessman named Bill McGuire happened to attend a Stars game. He didn't know much about soccer at the time. But he was taken by the fans' passion. After that 2012 season, he bought the club.

"We're going to take and honor what people have done in the past and build and grow on it," he said.

That showed in McGuire's first major decision. Prior to the 2013 season, the team adopted its current crest and changed its name to Minnesota United FC. The new name was meant to show the community, and its long soccer history, was together as one. However, almost immediately fans began calling the team the Loons, owing to their crest, which featured Minnesota's state bird.

SUPPORTERS' GROUPS

In 2004 a few fans decided to sit together at Thunder games. Today, that group is called the Dark Clouds, and it has more than 1,000 members. The Dark Clouds are Minnesota United's biggest supporters' group. Their motto is that wherever the team goes, "Dark Clouds Follow." True North Elite is United's other main group. Fans from these groups watch games from the south end of Allianz Field. They sing and chant and wave flags throughout. Outside of the games, these groups also sponsor programs to support the local community.

Bill McGuire purchased the club that became Minnesota United FC.

Fans celebrate the announcement of Minnesota United being welcomed to MLS.

With the new investment in the team, United took off. Attendance at the National Sports Center grew. The team played some games at the Metrodome in Minneapolis. Fans were drawn to the festive atmosphere and sense of community—and to star players such as Miguel Ibarra and Christian Ramirez.

This passion did not go unnoticed. On March 25, 2015, MLS commissioner Don Garber arrived in downtown Minneapolis to make an announcement. A group of fans in attendance might have said it best, though, to a song in the tune of "For He's a Jolly Good Fellow."

"The team that nobody wanted, the team that nobody wanted, the team that nobody wanted . . . is going to MLS!"

CHAPTER 3

LOON CALL

Miguel "Batman" Ibarra signed with Minnesota in 2012 after failing to find a spot in MLS. Christian "Superman" Ramirez joined the team in 2014, following a stint in the third division. The Californians became close friends while playing at the National Sports Center. They also became club icons in Minnesota's final seasons as a minor league club.

Ibarra, a crafty midfielder, won the 2014 Golden Ball as the league's best player. Coaches for the US national team noticed. They made Ibarra the first minor league player to earn a national team call up in nearly a decade. Ramirez, meanwhile, developed into a lethal striker in Blaine. He scored 50 goals from 2014 to 2016, earning two Golden Boots as the league's leading scorer in the process.

Miguel Ibarra helped the Loons make the transition to MLS.

As United prepared to move up to MLS, fans were eager for Batman and Superman to join them. Neither was certain to do so, though. Ibarra had outgrown the minor league Loons, and they had sold him to top Mexican team Club León in 2015. Ramirez had stayed with the Loons. However, several teams were eager to acquire him in 2017.

Minnesota's first two MLS signings were indeed longtime Loons: defenders Justin Davis and Kevin Venegas. Defender Brent Kallman and midfielder Ibson made the jump, too. But the big news came on January 5, 2017: Batman and Superman were back.

"They believe in this club, this community, and the people here in Minnesota," sporting director Manny Lagos said. "I think that should make everybody feel pretty proud."

Both players proved up to the task. On March 3, 2017, Ramirez received a pass atop the penalty area. Then he turned and sent a low, right-footed shot past the diving Portland Timbers' keeper. In the team's first MLS game, Ramirez had scored United's first MLS goal. He went on to score a team-high 14 goals that season. He had tallied seven more in 2018 before the team shocked fans by trading him to Los Angeles FC.

Christian Ramirez, *right*, keyed the United attack in their first MLS season.

Ramirez, *left*, and Ibarra celebrate Ibarra's game-winning goal against Colorado in April 2017.

Ibarra had a long history of proving people wrong. At 5-foot-7, he was a smaller player. His game didn't always fit into a traditional position. But with his work ethic, versatility, and playmaking, he always seemed to find a way back onto the field. He played in 86 MLS games over three seasons with United, 69 of them starts. Over those games he scored

11 goals and recorded 14 assists. However, the team decided not to re-sign Ibarra after the 2019 season, officially ending the Batman and Superman era.

EL CIENTIFICO DEL GOL

The fireworks started early on July 4, 2018, all thanks to Darwin Quintero. Eight minutes into the game against defending champion Toronto FC, Quintero nailed a long-range shot with the outside of his right shoe. The ball curved through the air, around goalie Clint Irwin, and into the goal.

On a humid evening in front of 20,559 fans at Minnesota's temporary home, TCF Bank Stadium, the show was only beginning. In the 52nd minute, he scored again, this time chipping it over Irwin with the inside of his right foot. And five minutes later, Quintero did it again—again on a looping right-footed chip over the helpless keeper. His goals, combined with one from Ibarra, led the Loons to

IBSON

Ibson had played for major clubs in Russia and his native Brazil before finding his way to Minnesota in 2015. The Loons kept him around when they moved to MLS. And it was there that the midfielder became a surprise sensation. Known for his creativity and flair, Ibson emerged as a key offensive player, appearing in 58 games over the 2017 and 2018 seasons. Coach Adrian Heath called Ibson the best player he'd ever worked with.

BANGERS ONLY

Defensive-minded players aren't often known for scoring lots of goals. Hassani Dotson is no exception. But when he did score in 2019, his goals always seemed to be spectacular. That earned him a calling card: Bangers Only. Not much had been expected of Dotson that season. He had been the 31st player selected in that year's draft. But his reliable play across 24 games as a fullback and defensive midfielder, plus his four "bangers," led to a breakout season for the rookie.

a memorable 4–3 win. They also marked the first hat trick in the team's MLS history.

"This is the fourth (hat trick) I've scored, but I can say with certainty that it is the best one I've scored," Quintero said, through a translator, afterward. "I hope there are a lot more goals to come."

Quintero had arrived in Minnesota earlier that season as the highest-profile signing in the young club's history. The 5-foot-5, 142-pound forward had been a star for some of Mexico's biggest teams. He had also suited up in 14 games for the Colombian national team.

With his small stature and elite dribbling skills, Quintero instantly became Minnesota's top playmaker. Nicknamed *"El Cientifico del Gol"* ("The Goal Scientist") he posted 21 goals and 20 assists across two seasons with the Loons.

Darwin Quintero (25) beats a New England defender and the goalkeeper to score for the Loons in 2018.

However, with his place in the lineup becoming less certain, the team traded Quintero to Houston before the 2020 season.

BE LIKE IKE

Ike Opara isn't the biggest defender. He's usually not the fastest player on the field either. But he's still plenty big and fast, and he's highly skilled, too. Everything the central defender does, he does well—and with grit. That's made him one of league's elite defenders.

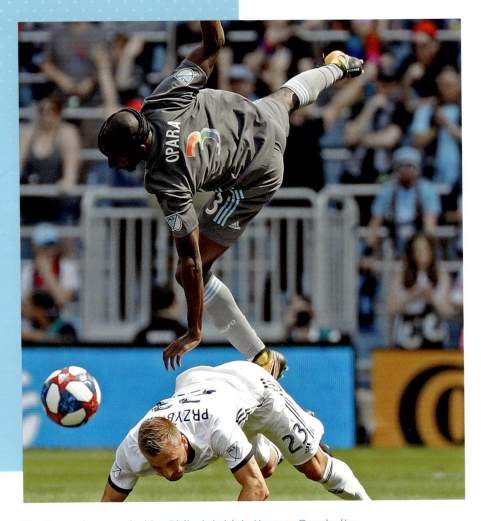

Ike Opara is upended by Philadelphia's Kacper Przybylko.

Opara's journey took some time. He was the third pick in the 2010 draft, but it wasn't until 2016 that he fully blossomed into a star. One year later, he was named MLS Defender of the Year while playing for Sporting Kansas City. After that, Opara asked for a raise. When Kansas City balked, Minnesota stepped in with a trade offer.

The move made a world of difference. After giving up 70 and 71 goals the previous two seasons, the Loons allowed just 43 in 2019. His efforts helped Minnesota reach the playoffs for the first time. Meanwhile, without Opara, Kansas City gave up 27 more goals than the year before and missed the playoffs for the first time in nine years.

SPREADING THEIR WINGS

Minnesota set out to sign Emanuel Reynoso in February 2020. The deal for the Argentinian midfielder finally wrapped up in September. That was just in time for Reynoso to come and drive the Loons into the playoffs.

The silky smooth playmaker quickly found his groove playing alongside Kevin Molino, Ethan Finlay, and Robin Lod. With Reynoso directing the offense, Minnesota finished 6–3–5 and then won two playoff games. He only seemed to get better as the season went on.

After recording one goal and seven assists in 13 regular-season games, Reynoso had back-to-back three-assist games in the playoffs. He added a goal and another assist in the conference final. No player in MLS history had recorded seven assists in a single playoffs. And he was just getting started.

CHAPTER 4

LEARNING TO SOAR

A steady snow fell on Minneapolis on March 12, 2017. It did little to dampen the enthusiasm at TCF Bank Stadium. Fans, bundled up in winter coats and team scarves wrapped around their necks, arrived from all directions. All were ready to cheer on Minnesota United in its first MLS home game.

In some ways, it was the perfect start for a Minnesota team. Workers had to shovel snow off the lines on the field. A special orange ball was used. And despite the 20-degree weather—the coldest kickoff in MLS history—one fan in the supporter's section bravely went shirtless.

The perfect start came quickly undone, though. Atlanta United had also joined MLS that season, and it had spent more money in putting together its first squad.

The weather was better suited for American football when the Loons hosted their first MLS home game.

The Minnesota supporters' section is called the Wonderwall after the anthem fans sing together after every victory.

That investment showed early and often. Atlanta went up 1–0 in the third minute. Then it added goals in the 13th and 27th minutes. Although Minnesota's Kevin Molino scored on a penalty kick soon after, Atlanta left the Twin Cities with a 6–1 victory. The 35,043 fans in attendance could see the home team still had a long way to go.

The loss followed a 5–1 drubbing at Portland in United's first MLS game. Although the Loons got their first points the next week in a 2–2 draw at Colorado, their following game was a 5–2 loss at New England. Finally, in its fifth game, Minnesota got its first win. After going down a goal against Real Salt Lake, the Loons came back to win 4–2. Afterward, "Wonderwall" blared from the speakers at TCF Bank Stadium for the first time.

The win didn't hide that the club had serious troubles on the defensive end, though. A trade with Colorado to pick up defender Marc Burch started to fix that. Burch and another former Rapids player, midfielder Sam Cronin, stepped right into the starting lineup. Michael Boxall, a central defender who played for the New Zealand national team, joined the Loons in July. Minnesota-born midfielder Ethan Finlay, a former MLS All-Star, arrived a month later.

Those moves helped shore up the squad. Boxall and Finlay would go on to become key contributors for years to come.

> ## BIG CROWDS
>
> The 2017 home opener marked the biggest crowd for a Minnesota soccer game since 1984. However, the 52,621 fans in 1984 were seeing a Beach Boys concert *and* a Minnesota Strikers game. Because of that, the team considered the state's single-game record to be 49,572 fans from a 1976 Kicks game. Before leaving TCF Bank Stadium for the smaller Allianz Field in 2019, United aimed to break that. Ultimately 52,242 fans came out to the 2018 season finale. However, the LA Galaxy beat the Loons 3–1.

Fiery goalkeeper Vito Mannone joined the Loons and helped spark their playoff run in 2019.

However, much of the play on the field that year was forgettable. As the Loons suffered through their blowout loss at New England early in the season, the TV camera focused in on some Minnesota fans. In front of them was a sign: "We're just happy to be here!" That summed up how a lot of fans felt during that first season, even as the Loons gave up an MLS-record 70 goals. When the defense was even worse the next season, however, the goodwill began to wear off. Fans were anxious to see some progress. Could the team really pull off its "three-year plan"?

THE THREE-YEAR PLAN

Fans had heard those three words often, but they were starting to doubt. Still, team management asked them to be patient. They were working toward 2019, Minnesota's third season, when Allianz Field would open. And in that third year, the team would be ready to compete.

United showed it was serious that offseason. First, the team signed Ozzie Alonso. He had been one of the league's best midfield destroyers for the Seattle Sounders. Then the Loons traded for Ike Opara, a former MLS Defender of the Year with Kansas City. The team also brought in goalie Vito Mannone on a loan. He had made a name for himself in England, including for a time in the Premier League. Together with new midfielder Ján Greguš and fullback Romain Métanire, both of whom had been playing in Europe, the new-look Loons were suddenly ready to shut down opponents.

After giving up 15 goals in their first seven games, the Loons gave up just three in their next six. The team recorded 11 shutouts on the season. It had just seven clean sheets combined in 2017 and 2018. Neighbors of Allianz Field were getting used to hearing "Wonderwall."

The Loons first showed they were contenders while playing in the US Open Cup. Dating back to 1913, the tournament is open to US teams of all levels. The format is simple: Win and move on, until only one team remains. With three wins, United moved on to the final four against Portland.

An amped-up crowd of more than 15,000 people showed up to Allianz Field on a Wednesday night. Minnesota had beaten the Timbers just three days earlier in league play. The rematch was intense. After trading goals in the first half, Portland put the pressure on early in the second. However, Mannone was able to hold them off. Then, in the 64th minute, forward Mason Toye broke loose to score the game-winning goal.

The final featured a familiar opponent: Atlanta United. A crowd of 35,709 came out to Atlanta's massive stadium. However, a slow start doomed the Loons, and they went on to lose 2–1.

Mason Toye celebrates his go-ahead goal against Portland in the US Open Cup semifinals.

Minnesota's Michael Boxall (15) sends a header just over the crossbar in the Loons' playoff defeat against the Galaxy.

United still had much to play for, though. The team went on to clinch its first playoff berth, and with the fourth-best record in the West, the Loons hosted a playoff game. Although Zlatan Ibrahimović and the LA Galaxy pulled out a 2–1 victory, Minnesota had shown it was ready to compete with anyone.

United showed that in 2020. The team got off to a 2–0 start before the COVID-19 pandemic shut down the season. When the league returned four months later for the MLS Is Back tournament, the Loons made a run to the final four.

The team faced many challenges when the regular season continued. An injury kept Ike Opara out after those first two games. Another early-season injury ended new goalie Tyler Miller's season, too. That forced players such as Boxall and goalie Dayne St. Clair to step up. And that's exactly what they did. But the true difference came when Argentinian playmaker Emanuel Reynoso arrived in September.

The Loons started clicking, and they went on to reach the playoffs as the No. 4 seed. This time they won their opener, beating Colorado at home, before upsetting rival Kansas City on the road. That set up a Western Conference title game at Seattle, the defending MLS champs. Minnesota appeared on its way to its first MLS Cup when it took a 2–0 lead. However, three Seattle goals in 18 minutes turned the tables. It was a disappointing loss for Loons fans, but one that showed just how far the team had come. WIth a passionate fanbase, one of the league's best stadiums, and an improving roster, the MLS era in Minnesota had officially taken flight.

TIMELINE

1976
The NASL's Denver Dynamos move to Minnesota and become the Kicks. The team enjoys great fan support in the early years and makes the league championship in its first season.

1990
Buzz Lagos founds the Minnesota Thunder as an amateur team. In 1995 the Thunder turn professional and join the A-League.

1999
The Thunder win the A-League championship, defeating the Rochester Raging Rhinos in the final.

2010
One year after the Thunder folded, the Minnesota Stars are formed, saving professional soccer in Minnesota for the time being.

2012
Local healthcare executive Bill McGuire buys the Minnesota Stars in November. The following spring the team takes a new identity as Minnesota United FC.

2015
MLS commissioner Don Garber announces that Minnesota United FC will join the league, bringing first-division men's soccer back to Minnesota.

2017
Christian Ramirez scores Minnesota's first MLS goal in a 5–1 loss at Portland on March 3. The Loons then fall 6–1 to Atlanta in the "Snow Opener" on March 12. United finally gets its first MLS win on April 1 against Real Salt Lake.

2019
The Loons win four games to qualify for the US Open Cup final. However, they fall 2–1 on the road in the title game against Atlanta United.

2019
On September 25, Hassani Dotson scores in the 90th minute to secure a 2–1 win over Sporting KC and clinch the Loons' first MLS playoff berth.

2020
Behind Argentinian playmaker Emanuel Reynoso, the Loons reach the playoffs again and make a run to the Western Conference final before losing a heartbreaker to the Seattle Sounders.

TEAM FACTS

FIRST SEASON

2017

STADIUM

TCF Bank Stadium (2017–18)
Allianz Field (2019–)

US OPEN CUP FINALS

2019

KEY PLAYERS

Osvaldo Alonso (2019–)
Michael Boxall (2017–)
Francisco Calvo (2017–19)
Ethan Finlay (2017–)
Ján Greguš (2019–)
Miguel Ibarra (2017–19)
Ibson (2017–18)
Vito Mannone (2019)
Romain Métanire (2019–)
Kevin Molino (2017–20)
Ike Opara (2019–)
Darwin Quintero (2018–19)
Christian Ramirez (2017–18)
Emanuel Reynoso (2020–)

KEY COACHES

Adrian Heath (2017–)

MLS DEFENDER OF THE YEAR

Ike Opara (2019)

MLS GOALKEEPER OF THE YEAR

Vito Mannone (2019)

MLS HUMANITARIAN OF THE YEAR

Matt Lampson (2018)

GLOSSARY

amateur
A person who plays a sport without getting paid.

assist
A pass that leads directly to a goal.

berth
A spot in a competition or a tournament earned through previous results.

clean sheet
Another term for a shutout in soccer.

defected
Abandoned one's country in favor of another.

destroyer
In soccer, a defensive midfielder who creates turnovers and keeps the opposing attack from getting organized.

draft
A system used to divide up new talent coming into a league.

rookie
A first-year player.

sporting director
The executive in charge of all soccer-related decisions for a club.

stoppage time
Also known as injury time, a number of minutes tacked onto the end of a half for stoppages that occurred during play from injuries, free kicks, and goals.

volley
To kick the ball while it's in the air.

MORE INFORMATION

BOOKS

Avise, Jonathan. *Sporting Kansas City*. Minneapolis, MN: Abdo Publishing, 2022.

Kortemeier, Todd. *Total Soccer*. Minneapolis, MN: Abdo Publishing, 2017.

Marthaler, Jon. *Ultimate Soccer Road Trip*. Minneapolis, MN: Abdo Publishing, 2019.

ONLINE RESOURCES

To learn more about Minnesota United FC, please visit **abdobooklinks.com** or scan this QR code. These links are routinely monitored and updated to provide the most current information available.

INDEX

Alonso, Ozzie, 4, 7, 8, 9–10, 39

Barath, Botond, 5
Boxall, Michael, 13, 37, 43
Burch, Marc, 37

Craig, Carl, 13
Cronin, Sam, 37

Danladi, Abu, 10
Davis, Justin, 26
Dotson, Hassani, 10–11, 30

Finlay, Ethan, 33, 37

Garber, Don, 23
Greguš, Ján, 39

Heath, Adrian, 10, 29

Ibarra, Miguel, 23, 24–26, 28–29
Ibrahimović, Zlatan, 43
Ibson, 26, 29
Irwin, Clint, 29

Kallman, Brent, 26

Lagos, Buzz, 16, 19
Lagos, Manny, 19, 26
Lod, Robin, 33

Mannone, Vito, 10, 39–40
McGuire, Bill, 20
Métanire, Romain, 39
Miller, Tyler, 43
Molino, Kevin, 33, 36

Opara, Ike, 31–33, 39, 43

Quintero, Darwin, 29–31

Ramirez, Christian, 23, 24–26
Reynoso, Emanuel, 33, 43

Sanneh, Tony, 19
St. Clair, Dayne, 43

Toye, Mason, 40

Venegas, Kevin, 26

ABOUT THE AUTHOR

Chrös McDougall is a sportswriter and children's book author who writes mostly about soccer and Olympic sports. A Minnesota native, he attended Thunder games at the National Sports Center growing up and is now a United season-ticket holder. He lives just across the river from Allianz Field in Minneapolis with his wife, son, and boxer, Eira.